SUZY HAS A SECRET

SUZY HAS A SECRET

By
S. Jackson, A. Raymond,
&
M. Schmidt

Disclaimer/Copyright

Suzy Has A Secret

This book teaches a child, ages four to eight years-old, about personal safety and body ownership. Children learn how to identify who safe adults are in a child's life. This book shows in positive and practical ways how parents, and educators, can talk to children about personal safety. Children learn about bad touch and good touch, and how their body belongs to them. Parents and educators can help children learn who the safe people are in their lives, and that they can always tell one of them about anything that may happen, and they aren't comfortable about. Using little bug fairies and fairy houses, ensures that children aren't scared when this story is read to them, or they read it on their own. Minimal illustrations used so that younger children don't become distracted by extraneous elements.

All text copyright © S. Jackson, A. Raymond, & M. Schmidt
Cover design by S. Jackson, A. Raymond, & M. Schmidt
Interior design © S. Jackson, A. Raymond, & M. Schmidt

Print history
First edition June 2016
Second edition published December 2017 (due to two women from Miami plagiarizing our first book of same title and galley)

ISBN-13: 978-0-692-12253-2 (S. Jackson, A. Raymond, & M. Schmidt)
ISBN-10: 198345401X
ISBN- : 9780692159200

Library of Congress Cataloguing-in-Publication Data

Suzy Has A Secret

2017 Silver Second Place Literary Titan December

Dedication

Always to Eli, Joshua and Noah who taught us so much about life on Earth;
To Rachel, Steven and Shadow who inspired this story to come to life;
To Austin, this book is for you;
Always to Matthew, my beloved husband, partner, and best friend in the entire world;
Always to Sarah, my beloved wife, partner, and best friend in the entire world;

Reviews

"Suzy Has A Secret" is a must read book for those with small children or for those that have little ones in their life. Children don't always know when or who to tell. We teach them to respect their elders and be quiet when asked; to behave and not to tattle. This needs to change! *"Suzy Has A Secret"* explains to children that we must always tell our parents or others when something doesn't feel right. I recommend this book highly. Susan Vance, Author

"Suzy Has a Secret" is a great resource in instructing children about good touch/bad touch. I think it is smartly written and developed, and easy for children to read. This is a difficult subject to tackle, and the authors have done a brilliant job. I would highly recommend this book. Kristina Ball, Author

As children, we've been taught to listen to our parents and to do everything they tell say us. We know how much they love us and they won't do anything to hurt us. One of these things concerns tattling on someone else who did something they shouldn't have done, because doing it wouldn't be a nice thing to do.

But what happens when a relative, like Uncle Bob, starts doing something he shouldn't and tell us to keep it a secret even from our parents. This is what Suzy has to deal with in this brief story when he starts touching her in places she somehow feels is wrong; she becomes scared and doesn't want to get in trouble for tattling on her uncle to her parents.

This creates a conflict in her young mind since her parents had also taught her that if something is bothering her she should come to them. When she tells her friend Lucy what's happening, Lucy's older brother tells Suzy to tell her parents and that she wouldn't get into trouble. Suzy follows his advice, tells her parents who respond by sitting down and talking to her about what Uncle Bob did to her.

Inappropriate touching is a sensitive, everyday occurring issue which parents need to discuss with their young child, and this book serves as marvelous beginning from which this discuss can begin. The book then gives parents ideas as to how to go about doing this. For trying to help parents, especially first-time young parents, in dealing with this important, sensitive issue, there's no way I can't give Ms. Jackson 5 STARS for her endeavor here. Mrs. D., Author

One Saturday afternoon Suzy's
mom and dad went out shopping.

Uncle Bob came over to
babysit her for a few hours.

Soon after they left, Uncle
Bob told Suzy he wanted to
play a new tickling game,
on the couch with her.

After tickling her tummy, Uncle
Bob touched Suzy's private area.

Uncle Bob told Suzy that this was a new secret.

Uncle Bob told Suzy that she was not to tell anyone about their new secret.

He told her that she
could not tell her
mommy or daddy.

Suzy did not feel right.
She did not like the
game they had played.

Suzy did not like the way Uncle Bob had touched her.

Suzy felt scared and she
did not know what to do.

Suzy wanted to cry because she was so scared of what had happened.

She was afraid of Uncle
Bob, and she was afraid
of getting into trouble
if she told anyone.

Later, Suzy and Uncle Bob
walked one block to the
school playground.

Uncle Bob was helping
Suzy on the swing.

Suzy's best friend, Lucy,
showed up and asked Suzy
to play on the slide.

Lucy saw that Suzy was sad,
quiet, and was crying.

Finally, Suzy told Lucy about the tickling game.

Lucy's older brother, Max,
heard what Suzy had said to her.

Max explained to Suzy
that what Uncle Bob
did to her was wrong.

Max told Suzy that she
had done nothing wrong
and that she would not
get into any trouble.

Max also told Suzy that
she needed to tell her
mommy and daddy.

Uncle Bob walked
Suzy back home.

Suzy's parents were home
and she told them about the
secret she had with Uncle Bob.

Suzy did not get into
trouble, and her mom
and dad helped Suzy to
talk about her afternoon.

For Parents and Educators

The following suggests ways in which you can help teach your child regarding good touch bad touch.

Children own their own bodies, and tell them that no one has the right to touch them unless it's okay with them. Children need to know that some of their body parts are theirs, and that they are private. This method helps children learn the difference between good touch versus bad touch. They need to know that they have a right to say no if they don't want their hand held and/or to be given a hug. May sure they know their body is theirs, and that permission must be given in order for a person, such as a doctor, is allowed touch them in places that are private.

Children have the right to refuse a hug, kiss or a touch from anyone, including those who they love. Children need to know that they can say "No" when they feel bad from a person touching them in a way they feel is bad touch. Remind children to run away from a bad touch, and to find a parent or trusted adult or teacher. Stress that they should persist until someone takes the matter seriously. Children may like hugs from a parent or sibling, but they need to know that they can tell others that they don't want a hug, if they feel the touch is bad to them. Teach children to understand that if a person touches them, and that touch feels bad to them, then they need to know that is what is called a bad touch. All children should be taught to trust their feelings when around or in a situation such as this, and that they can say "No."

Equally important is the fact that children need to know that a touch might feel good to them, yet if the touch falls in the "swim suit" area, then that touch is still a bad touch. This is a huge part of bad touch. Some children might think that this is how "daddy shows his love to me", or "Uncle Jack loves me when he touches me in my private places", and that trusted persons will try to convince the child that this is their way of showing love.

Always use age appropriate language. When the child is old enough, and they are curious about a part of their body, parents need to teach them the trued and correct names for those body parts. If children know the names of their private areas they will be able to tell a parent or educator about bad touch if it occurs.

Always keep your conversation light and comfortable. Comfortable children ask questions. Use bath time to talk with your child. This is the perfect time to show/tell/name their privates and that it's not for other people to look at or touch them in those areas. Children need to know and report when another person asks them to touch their parts or to look at them.

Use the swimsuit rule and tell children that the areas of their body that their swimsuit covers are their private areas and that no one should be looking or touching those areas. Children need to know that they can tell a parent or a trusted adult, that someone touched them in their privates.

Sometimes, the abuser will start with stroking a child's hair or neck. Even though these areas aren't private ones, if the child doesn't like this touch, they can say no, and tell their parents. Children need to know and be able to tell their parent of any touch anywhere that they don't like.

Explain safe touch to your child and tell them that, sometimes, they might have to visit a doctor, and that, parents and doctors might have to touch them. Give them examples of doctors listening to the child's heart, touching their tummy, and giving them a shot.

Abusers use secrets as their main tactic with children. Teach your child the difference between good and bad secrets. If the secret is not telling someone what their birthday present is, then they know it is a good secret. However, if a child feels sad, anxious, or fearful about a secret, they need to be taught that it is a bad secret. They need to tell a parent, teacher or a policeman, and feel safe in doing so.

Children must be able to talk with a trusted adult, and that the adults need to allow for the child to tell them, and to listen to what the child has to say. Children need to be taught how to go for or who to go to in telling their story, when their parent(s) aren't around. It is important to have a safety network in place and that the child and the adults know their roles.

Whether you live in a city or smaller rural area, known perpetrators live in your area. A list of registered offenders for your zip code can be found online at your state's website. Teach your child the basic rules such as to never get into a car with a stranger, never accept gifts, money, candy, or invitations from a stranger.

Unfortunately, in many cases, the perpetrator is someone known to the child. As such, it is especially hard for young children to understand that someone who knows them could abuse them.

Children need to be taught that adults in their school are able to help them, and that they can talk to any adult in charge.

What do you do if you suspect abuse has occurred? First, don't be angry with your child, and make sure they don't feel like they did anything wrong or bad. Be careful with your questions, and keep them simple. If the child sees you angry or sad, they might not tell you the whole story. Children need to know that you will do something about this, and then you need to report this to the proper authorities, as well as a child specialist who can help them with their feelings.

Author Bio

S. Jackson is a retired registered nurse; a member of the Catholic Church, and has taught kindergarten Catechism; she has worked in various capacities for The American Cancer Society, March of Dimes, Cub and Boy Scouts, (son, Noah, is an Eagle Scout), and sponsored trips for high school children music. She loves all forms of art but mostly focuses on the visual arts; such as amateur photography, traditional, and graphic art as her disabilities allow.

A. Raymond is a member of the Catholic Church, and has helped his wife with The American Cancer Society, March of Dimes, Cub and Boy Scouts, and sponsored children alongside his wife on music trips. He devotes his spare time to fishing, reading, playing poker, Jeeping, and travel adventures with his wife.